CW01665622

Karolin

Let There Be Time

Michael Terence Publishing

First published in paperback by
Michael Terence Publishing in 2020
www.mtp.agency

ISBN 9781800940000

To Michael Terence Robinson

"See you in Heaven, my friend."

Prologue

My dear reader,

I choose to address you directly because there are no words for me to express the gratitude I feel for your time and willingness to read my thoughts. As you may know, alcoholism has deep roots in my family; my father was (maybe still is) an alcoholic for as long as my mother can remember. He had a great job and lost it, had excellent health - all gone. Rumours are going around the city that he's homeless now and that would not surprise me. I haven't seen him for over twenty-five years, and I have no intentions of doing so! Why would I? He missed out on all of my life and genuinely, have no respect for men that beat their wives, abandon their children and blame it all on drinking.

My mother just got sober after wasting thirty years of her life at 'the bottom of a bottle'. Thirty years of self-harm, domestic abuse and no self-worth! She went from one lousy decision to another. From being in abusive relationships over and over again, repeating the ritual of self-destruction. You'd think

I know better than that, wouldn't you? Sadly, you would be wrong…

It's now been three years since I've drunk alcohol! I went from a multi-thousand Euro debt to owning my own home, having a successful business and a substantial stash of savings. I even own a boat, for crying out loud! But I am quite sorry that I wasted ten years of my youth and my hard-earned cash on a 'party' that lasted far too long!

I will tell you my story and explain to you why and how come I chose sober living. Unquestionably, it changed my life! I've never felt more conscious and more fortunate than I am now. I did not spend any money on therapy treatments, medication, nor attended a 'twelve-step program'. It is my hope that maybe you can learn from my slips and you do not need to go through all of this embarrassment! There is an appropriate time in everyone's life to experience a little bit of booze, attend a few parties, and there is nothing wrong with that! As long as you know when to stop and you do not put yourself into harm's way. But that's not what happened to me.

So, there I was, laying on my dirty bathroom floor. From the corner of my eye, I could see the dust balls under the basin unit, wriggled with some hair because I hadn't cleaned in a really long time! I moved into this gorgeous penthouse that overlooks the Mediterranean Sea over a year ago. It's an idyllic place! The small, quiet country-side village, with the close-knit community. The breathtaking sunrises and magnificent sunsets.

I can smell the vomit and start to realise that my lose ponytail is bathing in it. I haven't eaten anything solid in days, so the puke is just an acidic foam. There's this itchy sensation from dried blood all over my mouth and chin… I try to scratch, but a sharp pain immediately widens my eyes! I see my small puppy lurking around, trying to wake me up because he hasn't been fed since yesterday morning. He licks my face, and I am getting disgusted by this 'picture'.

What happened last night? I think to myself. I do remember. It was a gorgeous, sunny day. The summers here can get really hot! But yesterday we had a breeze. I had a '*Skype* date' with my gal-pal from Ireland and a couple of long-distance 'cheers'. I've had the joy to live in various countries, so I am blessed to have friends all over the place. But if you want to maintain the friendships, regular 'check-ins' are necessary. Also, there is nothing more satisfying than a good gossip session, especially when there's a heartbreak involved! I remember having some drinks, but then it's all just a dark spot in my brain. Maybe not just a spot, no, it is more like a hole. Because it is not just yesterday that I don't remember. It is not easy to admit, that it became quite a norm; I drink, I get tipsy, then I go to buy more wine, beer or vodka and drink till I cannot walk. And usually, I don't remember anything… Zilch… Nada… The only positive note is that I get too drunk to text or call. Otherwise…

I slowly peeled myself off the floor, holding onto the sink and I looked in the mirror… *Who is this person? Why am I doing this to myself?* The unwashed eye makeup is giving that extra-dramatic appearance, and the one remaining false eyelash hanging on its glue residue making me look like a cartoon character. When you binge drink as often as I do, vomiting becomes like the grand finale of the night, so waterproof mascara is definitely recommended!

Stumbling into the kitchen, I see two 200ml empty bottles of vodka. The *Absolut* is my choice, mainly because they have these exciting flavours and you think you are posh! They make extraordinary flavours these days: caramel, tangerine, grapefruit, raspberry, strawberry, blueberry, teaberry, vanilla, black currant, chilli pepper, cherry, apple, cinnamon, coffee, chocolate, cranberry, peach, pear, passion fruit, pomegranate, plum, mango, banana, pineapple, coconut, mint, melon, rose… The list goes on and on!

There is a crystal-clean ashtray on the table, but the ashes and cigarette butts are everywhere. I smoke a lot when I drink. But strangely I smoke only menthol cigarettes. I guess it makes me believe that it tastes fresh… But how fresh can it be after three packs? My heart skips a beat just a little when I notice the laptop covered in the energy drink. My computer is my everything! I do not own a TV nor a stereo. Therefore, my *MacBook* is the cinema, the concert arena and the shopping mall. It also holds all of my precious possessions - pictures. Since I've never backed up in my whole life, you can imagine the paralysing despair I was in. I press the sticky keys, but it is dead. I quickly plug in the power supply, in an attempt to resuscitate, but it's too late.

The dog's bowl is as dry as my mouth, so I slowly move around the kitchen, pouring some dry food and water for the puppy. I saunter; otherwise, the stomach might get upset, and I'll get sick again. I touch my mouth - it is painful to move. Once I spot the dining chair laying sideways on the floor and drops of blood, I put two and two together. I guess I fell. Gently, with the tip of a cotton bud dipped in water, I am trying to remove the blood from my face. If there were any vodka left, I would dunk the bud in it - like they show in films. I press the tip of my tongue against the top lip, and I can see it is split, luckily my teeth are okay.

The worst part about living in a Mediterranean climate is the heat. It can go from 25° up to 34° in a matter of an hour and when you are hungover, the high temperature does not help. I decided to switch on the fan and spend the rest of the day in bed hating myself, asking the same questions over and over again: *How did I let this get so far? Why can't I just stop? Why is it always the blackout that I am after?* We all swear not to touch the Devil's Nectar once we feel like shite, but as soon as the hangover wears off, we are back for more. Literally more because if two years ago one 200ml bottle would have put you to bed, now you need two of them. And then in another five years… well, you get my point!

I knew I had to do something. This whole unstoppable drinking would destroy me, and it is destroying me already! Shot after shot, one glass after another, pint after pint - with every single fall, burn and lost consciousness, the true essence of me is disappearing! I walk the streets at night, drunk and alone, looking for an open shop. I live from paycheck to paycheck, with no money to spare and debts that would take years to clear.

It's not who I am, and it's not who I want to be…

Alcohol was always a massive part of my life from a very young age. My biological father was/is an alcoholic, my mother has been sober for the past ten years, but she was an alcoholic for the majority of my life. I never considered that alcoholism could be passed on to your children, but I do understand that exposure to it played a significant role in my upbringing. My father had a fantastic job as a welder - for those times it was an extremely well-paid job. My mom is still a smashingly excellent hairdresser. Just like thousands of other parents, they got up in the morning, went to work, came back home and drank. I guess they call them 'functioning alcoholics'.

Frankly, I used to get excited when I saw my parents drinking! They were less strict, more relaxed and would give me cash for candy! I could not wait till they had another party; their friends would come over and they would give me even more cash for candy (I had a 'sweet' childhood). Back where I am from, that is how adults used to deal with their kids. They'd give you money so you would fuck off; otherwise, we'd sit around the table, nag them with some childish nonsense and they would be forced to watch their language and supposedly pay attention to our gibberish.

The music used to play till the early hours of the morning, no neighbour ever complained because they were drunks just like my parents were. Misery loves company! I missed out on nursery school a lot because they were too hungover to take me. I would stay at home and watch television in bed - all day!

And during one of those parties was when, for the first time, I tried alcohol. I think I was four or five years old, the older kids of my parents' friends sneaked some of the cherry liqueur off the adults' table, and we all took sips in the bathroom.

"Come on. You go first, it's your home," one lad shoved the nearly empty bottle into my chest.

"Oh, I don't know, you guys, what if it's not good?" I hesitated.

"Just drink it! Hurry, they might come looking for us!" the kids rushed me.

I carefully took one small sip. It had a rich but very acidic taste, and my mouth felt like it was on fire. Then my throat started to burn. I was not planning on taking another sip, but I did. Not because I liked it, but we were doing this together and it is nice to be involved, included, engage with others just like my parents did with their friends! It did puzzle me because I saw the effect on others; adults were laughing, telling jokes and having fun, the older kids with red-hot cheeks were giggling and pushing each other around, but me - I just felt woozy. Brushing my tongue against my rotten baby teeth, I could only question the reasoning behind the drinking!

Soon enough, my parents' drinking was not as fun as it used to be; they drank more and more, and the more they drank the more often they got into fights - and for some reason, I used to get punished. We lived in a small studio flat. So as not to fight in front of me, they used to lock me out! That's right. They would dress me up, take me into the hallway and lock the doors. I used to sit on the staircase for hours, and if was not too cold, I would go outside. Sometimes neighbours would spot me lurking at night and take me inside their apartments.

They were never legally married, so the 'separation' or a 'break-up' happened after he grievously injured her. My father used to steal her money to buy some cheap, home-made schnapps from the local gipsies and when on one of those occasions, she hid the cash, my father broke half of my mother's fingers and told her:

"Now you'll be a useless hairdresser!"

The years that followed brought even more pain and trauma, which I am not going into now, since I believe you've read in my first book *Let There Be Light*, but if you didn't, well, do it…

I guess I accepted the alcohol as a normal part of adulthood because I saw it everywhere! I grew up with commercials on the television about booze; the grown-ups used to allow me to dip my pinky finger in a glass of dessert wine, some pharmaceutical companies, believe it or not, put alcohol in a kids cough syrup, for the love of God! I remember asking my mother once:

"Mummy, why do you drink wine all the time?"

"It helps me sleep," she said. So, given this answer, I was bringing her a mug-full of wine every evening. I was trying to take care of her.

Nowadays, there is more and more research done about the repetitive exposure and what effect it has on the young mind. But I was born in the Soviet Union, dear, and back then nobody gave a rat's behind about such things! Please, do not think I am making excuses, but to me, alcohol was a normal thing to encounter. I mean, just look around you; every comedy film portrays partying as a *must* in a young person's life, with some trashy pop music in the background, and loads of sexy women. Every TV show has an episode with a scene of somebody coming home from a long day at work and announcing:

"Oh, God, I need a drink!"

At the restaurants they 'sell' you the idea of drinking all wrapped up in a posh attitude; the pubs and bar have the ability to describe their brew selection if a mouth-watering way. They've invented various ways to serve alcohol: shots, mixers, frozen. They will pour the damn thing inside a huge pineapple, stick two straws in it and will sell it to you as a 'couples treat'! The only reason they invented cocktails is that they disguise the terrible taste, so you're actually able to drink it! And if you go to the supermarket, the booze is cheaper than a slice of wild-caught salmon... Society has made alcohol acceptable and accessible; so, do not blame yourself for falling into those traps! Blame yourself, for staying in them...

Let's all just admit that most of us got properly drunk for the very first time back in our teenage years. I guess it's that rebellious momentum, the peer pressure, wanting to be *cool* and to mimic the adults. To get alcohol, back then, used to be so easy. All you had to was go to the same shop where your parents bought their booze and pretend that you are buying for them. It was extra helpful if you look innocent and make a cute voice:

"Good day, my mommy asked if you can give me a box of that white wine she always gets here. You know, the one with a little tap." Small details like that would indicate that the merchandise came from this kiosk!

"Oh, yes, of course. But tell her next time to write a note." No sales lady ever questioned me; I just passed the cash and collected the wine.

The note was some ridiculous invention for the shops which allowed them to sell liquor to kids. Basically, you sent your child to a store with, written on a small (clean) piece of paper, something like:

> *Dear salesgirl,*
>
> *Please, sell to my daughter a bottle of Green Label white wine and a small pack of all-purpose flour.*
>
> *Mother*

I swear I am not making this up!

It was a Friday afternoon, and that evening school was holding its monthly disco. I was fourteen years old, which was old enough to enter. My friends and I gathered our lunch money, and it was my task to provide the 'supplies'. I went to the same kiosk, got a bottle of vodka - not a challenge for a *regular customer.*

"Why, did she not write you a note?" the salesgirl asked.

"Erm… My mommy does not feel well today," I replied.

"Oh, I see… I understand. Here, take it," she passed the bottle wrapped in a shopping bag - for security reasons.

We decided to meet a few blocks away from the school. A half-litre bottle of vodka and a small can of orange juice was provided by me. Other kids had some stolen cigarettes from their parents, but I wasn't interested. We took turns; swig after a swig. The taste of vodka was disgusting! It made me gag with every swallow, but twenty minutes later I felt a pleasant tingle in my body. I was feeling warm and delighted. We finished the bottle and slowly walked towards the school. No teacher was guarding the door, so we walked in without any inspection, even though it was apparent that some of us were *too happy*. With no shame I'll admit that back in those days I was a huge fan of Britney Spears - I mean, totally crazy about her. The walls in my room were covered with posters of her; I knew all the dance routines. So, when the deejay - a senior school student played her song - the dance floor was mine! I was putting on a show: little, fourteen-year-old dancing in front of the whole school. People were gathered around, cheering and clapping. Once I'd finished my *performance*, some older schoolboys start to approach me, asking to dance. I felt like I was noticed; I was important and attractive.

Next day, lying in bed, watching morning cartoons with a bowl full of cereal, I was wondering: *How come I was so awesome last night, but never before? Was it the vodka? It must be…*

After that evening, I was drunk every other Friday. My outfits got more and more revealing, up to the point where, on one very particular evening, as I was trying to get into school disco, a teacher refused to let me in. He told me to go home and change. Obviously, I was not going to do that, since I had my *buzz* on - I wanted to party! My mates, being totally loyal, agreed to leave the disco and try to find somewhere we could all hang out. We ended up going to one of their homes since the parents were out. Having no more money for booze, we decided to ransack the cupboards and found some wine, which without even asking I chugged down, leaving my partners in crime with just a few sips. And then all got weird…

I did not feel right. My head was spinning, and my eyes felt heavy. Somebody was assisting me and walked me into the next room. As I was slammed on the bed, I felt like throwing up. I could tell that somebody was next to me, stroking my bare legs, placing hands under my short skirt, touching my crotch. But I was too heavy and tired to move, I could barely speak. Trying to mumble something I turned on my belly and passed out. Two hours later, the guy whose home we were crashing at woke me up and told me that his parents were on their way back. We must all leave! Now! I noticed that my skirt was lifted to my waist, and my panties felt twisted. In autopilot mood, I walked back home.

I looked at my mother passed out on the sofa in the living room with the TV still on. The empty beer cans on the carpet and her glasses hanging on the tip of her nose gave me the inkling that she may have visited *the kiosk*!

I went back to school the following Monday to find out that some guy had told everybody he fingered me and that I should start to shave. There was graffiti-type writing at the bus stop:

Karolina is a whore!

One of the teachers heard the rumours and took me to the principal's office. The head of the school, the beacon of the students, was an old hag. She told me I was a disgrace to the school, that I had no morals and sent me home with the note.

> *Valeria,*
>
> *Please come see me as soon as you can. I would like to discuss your daughter's inappropriate behaviour regarding boys. I have also been informed that your payment for Karolina's lunch this semester has not been received.*
>
> *Thank you,*
>
> *Principal Hagel*

I threw away the note and never gave it to my mother. I was beyond mad and angry! And the embarrassment was pushing me into a place where I was afraid to go back to school. So, I ended up skipping classes for the month and instead started to hang out with the kids I shouldn't. Those kids were from broken families, with dysfunctional attitudes and had zero judgment! And that was precisely what I needed: the comfort that only comes from non-judgemental understanding.

Ever since that incident, I've praised the Lord that back in my teen years there was none of that social media stuff, nor smartphones. Nobody was forced to be exposed for the whole community, city, country or world to see! Whatever shite you did was just a temporary subject. And so was my fingering event. Soon it was all forgotten, and my name on the bus stop graffiti was replaced by some other girl's name. Life went on.

You would be please to know that I got my act together! Well, for the first part of the day. I went to school and did well; did my homework as required - I was an honourable student. In the evenings, I hang out with kids from another school that I'd got to know during my 'bunking' days. Those kids, just like me, came from some sort of dysfunctional background, divorced parents, drunks, jobless bums. So, we had some kind of compassion for each other. Every evening we got drunk, we smoked and talked about how unfair life was and that our parents deserved to die. Most of the 'crew' were goths, (well back then we did not have any other sub-category), and a few were into rap culture. But surprisingly we all get along really well, because if you think about it: rock music and rap - they all come from a place of hurt. And yes, you have guessed it right - I said nothing about Britney Spears…

During one of those self-pity evenings, the youngest member of our group started to tell us the story about his cousin. That his uncle, the father of his cousin, was selling illegal cigarettes and other tobacco products, and that in their home there were boxes and boxes piled up and he knows where the keys are hidden.

"I swear! The boxes are just laying around, everywhere," the young fellow said.

"How much you think we could get for one carton?" the other boys were discussing.

"My mother buys a carton of cigarettes from the gipsies, for ten," I intervened, "I am sure we could sell for less and still make a profit since they're stolen."

Of course, we had to do something about it!

The ingenious plan was to get inside the house, grab a few boxes of contraband and sell it. So, we did it just that! But the greatest robbery was short-lived as a few days later we were all picked up by the cops from the park bench, where we used to hang out, and taken to the police department. Officers took us one by one to separate rooms for interrogation. I did not say a word; I'd watched too many episodes of *The Sopranos*, I knew it was the right thing to do. The young fellow, whose cousins house we robbed, spilled all the beans and since he was thirteen or so, was released without any consequences. The rest of us had to face the day in court.

The whole school was shocked when the news reached the teachers; they could not believe it. I took part in it. I was such a good girl…

"Karolina, I cannot believe you would do such a thing! What were you thinking? It's those bloody kids, isn't it? They influenced you, yes?" my teacher was asking.

"Yes… I don't know. I'm sorry," with a mumbled excuse I left the classroom.

Coming to clean to my mom was easy because I lied. I told her that I was never inside the house, that I was only on look-out, and she bought it. I gave an improvised speech about how the older kids bullied me into doing it and that she knew I would never do anything like that. The only thing she asked, was:

"Is there going to be a fine?"

I said no, and she was okay with the rest. During sentencing, I was the only one from the 'gang' to address the courtroom. I gave a well-rehearsed monologue about how sorry I was, and they bought it. (Adults fall way too easily for teenagers' manipulative, insincere remorse). Since I'd never had any criminal record, and I was academically progressive, the judge gave me one year of house arrest. The remainder of my 'gang' were sent to the Juvenile Detention Centre for sixteen months (mainly due to the fact that all of them were over sixteen years old).

Now that I think back, I praise the Sweet Jesus and all other *Last Supper* attendees! Thoughts of what my life could have been if I was to be sentenced to juvenile time as well, were not promising me a bright future. Those troubled youth institutions in Lithuania, most likely, used to be used for some KGB training. It was a rough place to be in!

On June 1st, 2005, I started my one-year house arrest sentence. I was not allowed to leave my home between ten o'clock in the evening and six in the morning. Every night, at random times, a police officer would come over, and I had to sign some 'house-minding' papers. I don't think my mother even realised that those visits were taking place, since she was out partying most nights.

You'd think this whole situation would shake me into my senses, right? Well, every time a police officer used to come for my signature, the moment they were gone, I was out of the door because, remember, there was still one remaining kid left from our 'gang' that understood my life.

"Are you mad?" he asked me, passing the roll-up.

"No, it's okay man, we're fine," I bumped my fist into his cheek.

"How about the rest? Do you talk to them?"

"Cobra did send me a letter, asking to send some cigarettes, but I won't," I exhaled the smoke.

Okay, so he ratted all of us out, but I had no other friends. He was a young boy, and because he was a boy, I think the cops went extra on him and he just 'cracked'. But regardless of the past, we developed a big sister-little brother bond, continue to drink and smoke, because life is all about disappointment. His classmates used to tease him about me being his girlfriend, and he liked it. My classmates used to tease me about him being my boyfriend, and I did not like that at all!

Sadly, nearly a year later my 'little brother's' parents decided to move to another city, and I never heard of him again. Myself, I finished the house arrest deal with *flying colours* and decided to straighten my life. Finished high school and got into university.

During my freshers' year at the university, I was offered a fully-funded place on the student exchange program in the Netherlands. I told the student councillor that I needed some time to think, but as soon as I got home, I knew what to do.

My mother and I were growing further and further apart. Her drinking became so severe that she was now physical with me. I don't know how many times she would stumble into my room demanding for some money that allegedly I stole from her, screaming that she should have aborted me and that she wished I would get kidnapped, raped and sold to prostitution. And precisely the same story unfolded that day. She started to punch me and kick me - I couldn't be around her anymore. I had to leave. The next day I signed the paperwork, and two months later, I was on a plane to the Netherlands.

I do not know how it is was in the rest of the Netherlands, but the academy I was placed in required no classroom attendance whatsoever. You got your tasks via email, and you delivered them in print. You can only imagine that with all this spare time on my hands, and the cash I got from the European Union, there was not much else to do than to look for friends. (I am sure that the European Union was not happy the way I spent the money they gave me for being a 'good student', but books were expensive, and beer was cheap.)

Oh, funny story about this exchange program. So, when I was filling in the necessary paperwork work, I was eminent about the fact that I do not speak, nor write in English. I had German and Russian as my foreign languages. God only knows why my university placed me in an English-only academy! *Google Translate* was nothing like it is now! We are talking thirteen years ago. So, I had to translate everything into Lithuanian, just to be able to understand the task. Then, bit by bit, type everything in in Lithuanian and translate it into English. Every word: one by one, page after page, essay after essay…

So, for those people that were endlessly *trolling* me on the internet about my lack of English grammar and terrible spelling: 'Idi na chuj!' Now, google that, you monolingual twat!

After the first month of being abroad, I started to feel lonely. I had another five months to go, but I seriously doubted if I would last that long. Going from bar to bar, meeting strange guys that were not there to be my friends... I was lost.

Every now and then, the next-door neighbours of the apartment I was renting - an amazing Dutch family was asking me over for a happy hour. The mother was a Hip Tomboy style that rode a Harley to work, and the father was this intellectual that smoked Cubans and knew something about every topic. They had two sons, a bit older than me, but we all grew more and more fond of each other. Soon enough, I used to spend every day at their house, having a drink, dinner, watching films. Spending most of my time with them, I came to understand that having a drink is perfectly fine. But getting drunk it is not! They explained to me about the traditions and the culture; we travelled around the country. I felt a bond, a connection, and I still do till this very day!

I did not even see it coming - my time in the Netherlands was nearly over. One evening, feeling genuinely sad, I burst into tears and told them that I had nobody waiting for me at home. They had a little previous knowledge of my story, but that day I told them everything. To my shock, I was given an *open invitation* to stay with them. For as long as I felt like, their home was my home too. I could not believe it! Complete strangers offering me this fantastic gift, whereas at home there's a drunk out of her skull mother that did not, as it happens, bother to ring me once in six months.

There was nothing to think about. I was in! Till this very day, I tell my mom that going to study abroad was the most beautiful thing that happened to me. Otherwise, we would never be able to communicate. Not on a physical level, nor spiritually or emotionally. I was ready to cut her out of my life!

I flew back to Lithuania, only to deliver the paperwork to the university.

"Are you sure about this?" the counsellor asked me as I was leaving the office.

"No," I said. I'd dropped out with only two years left before graduating.

As I was packing my remaining clothing, I looked around thinking if I would miss this place. But it was never a home. For a place to be home, you must feel love and care. This place had only the stench of cigarettes and old garbage in the air. The goofy pictures of my friends were nicely framed on the wall; the CD collection, random bits and pieces that I'd gathered throughout the years from places I'd visited, and things that people gave me, as to remember them. I left all that behind. It all looked like a child's room, and I was about to grow up. So, I closed my mother's apartment door feeling sad but hopeful!

I went back to the Netherlands. I went away in search of a home.

Hospitality. I genuinely believe that there is no other industry that runs on drugs and alcohol so freely and out in the daylight. If you ever worked in catering, you know exactly what I mean.

So, I landed my very first job in the Netherlands at a four-star hotel in Amsterdam. I was nervous out of my head, but the manager that hired me told me:

"You have that flair."

Back then, I did not even know what the heck that word meant, but I took it, and I ran with it.

The level of pressure working in catering is crazy. No, seriously - there is a special place in heaven for all of us that worked in hospitality, especially in the food and beverage division. When you are a waitress, you get blamed for basically everything: the lighting in the restaurant, the deejay, the wobbly tables, the last song that deejay played, the food, the prices, the current song that deejay is playing, the taxes and for that song that deejay forgot to play. So, obviously, after a night like that, what do you do? Go out for a drink with your colleagues - because only they can understand what it is like. Maybe it's human nature to associate yourself with like-minded people. Perhaps we are pack animals that only thrive in a paired environment.

"Are you going to Maggie's party tomorrow?" my colleague asked.

"Who's Maggie?"

"The girl from housekeeping. She lives in this sweet top-floor apartment by the Vondelpark with a huge terrace," he explained.

"I don't know, I have a breakfast shift on Sunday," I hesitated.

"Oh, come on! It's not like we're landing aeroplanes here. You should come. It will be fun!"

Soon I was a regular at Maggie's!

Alcohol in catering is the number one ingredient when it comes to team bonding. And it works! If employees get along, they work more productively; sometimes they, believe it or not, work harder because they know, at the end of the shift they can all hang out and let it hang. The kitchen staff are usually all about drugs. Cocaine keeps them alert during the ten-hour shifts. Kitchen staff would rarely join in for a boozy night out. They simply cannot mix drugs with alcohol. Some of them do, but then end up crashing for days. Just to be clear - I am not talking about all-inclusive Chinese buffet restaurants. I'm talking about high-end service places, where your *Tripadvisor* comment can cost someone their job.

I used to party six nights a week and rest one. When you are in your twenties, your body can handle things like that. It is perfectly fine, that's what the twenties are for. And so, I spent the most beautiful three years working at that beautiful hotel, in the beautiful restaurant with my beautiful colleagues.

By law, in the Netherlands, if an employee has worked for three consecutive years in the same company, he or she must be given a permanent contract, and most of the businesses don't like to do that. So, they offer you to take a three-month break and then come back again, or not and start with a new contract of employment. I was so enraged that I wasn't offered the permanent contract that I gave them a middle finger and applied to work for our biggest competitors at the time.

"Karolina, you are such a hard worker. For you to find a job elsewhere will be easy," said my supervisor.

"But I love it here. I've worked like a maniac for three years, and now you are telling me I am no longer needed, because of some stupid technicality?" I was raging.

"I am sorry, but they don't have any more permanent contracts left to assign for this year."

I went on and got a job at the five-star hotel just a few blocks away from my previous work and *gee-whiz* things were different there. Yes, the business was the same; the plates were still round, and the stove was hot, but it was a different level and much more pressure. I needed knowledge that I hadn't gained before: the world's most luxurious ingredients, wines, techniques - as waiting staff, you were expected to know the cooking process as well.

After-shift drinks weren't doing it for me anymore. My tolerance for high amounts of alcohol was growing. And the more I needed to get to 'that level', the worse the day after was. So, to fix the hangover, I got into the habit of getting buzzed before work. Just two, three alcopops before my shift started, it gave me a good energy boost and you can say whatever you like, but I felt on point! That little tipsy feeling was giving me the right attitude; I was over the top polite to snobs, and cheeky to our regulars. I was cracking jokes and being attentive. Day after day and the tips were flooding my pockets! I was the new *Maggie*! I organised the parties, I was the one to include people from other departments, I was a matchmaker, a listener and a 'mom'. I was the one that bought the drinks and paid for the taxi.

"It's on me, you guys!" I yelled out through the pumping music at the bar, whilst handing over my back card to the waitress.

"Oh, girl, you're the best!" one of my colleagues shouted back and kissed me on the cheek.

It was nice to feel important. I guess that is why money equals power. When you have cash, people fancy you, and if they fancy you, there's a big chance you can manipulate them in your favour.

But I never did anything as such. I just enjoyed having them around me! Looking up to me! As if I was somewhat better.

My colleagues adored me, and with the high-ranked reviews, my manager was offering me a promotion! I was on fire! I was popular! And you would not dare to tell me that it is all because of alcohol; I was the door, and my *Bacardi Breezer* was the key!

"You are on fire, girl!" my manager tapped me on the shoulder, "table five is extremely pleased with you tonight."

"That's what I do, boss," I replied with a cocky expression and pouted lips.

"Oh, okay! I love the attitude. Keep it up, Karolina. I have great plans for you!" he mumbled quietly, not wanting my peers to overhear.

I would wake up with uneasy feeling and fix myself a cocktail and on the way to work sip on an alcopop while comfortably sitting on the train. Then, during my shift, I'd pop out for a pint at the bar next door. And as soon as the shift was over, it was me that rounded up everybody and led them to the next 'watering-hole'.

I spent months continually being under the influence. Whether it was a strong spirit or just a sissy cocktail - it did not matter. Until it did…

Since childhood, I felt like I was stripped of the right to be a daddy's girl. There was never an influential man figure in my life that would assure me of my worthiness. I never had a father that would chase the persuading boys away from me. Or to sit a potential boyfriend down and tell him:

"If even a hair falls off my daughter's head, I swear to all that's dear to me, I will murder you..."

I will never have a father to walk me down the aisle when the time comes. And I will never get that feeling of seeing my son on his grandfather's lap. So, yes, I do have daddy issues, but they only come out to creep after the third drink. And that is the time when an ordinary loser can have his chance, because once a daddy-issues-filled chick is hammered, she doesn't care!

I never thought of myself as *an easy girl.* But once I had a bit too much to drink, I start to feel the *need* for company. The situation was so bad that it was not enough I used to offer to pay for the whole bill, but also offered myself on a plate! Feel free to pass on your judgment… No wonder guys used to call me up all the time - I provided the company, the drinks and the shag!

But for me, it has never been about sex; it was the company that I used to seek. The 'let's pretend we are a couple' part that I was interested in. And yes, those moments sometimes led to the one-night stands and yes, I regretted it in the morning. But you saw those films where they meet in the bar, get cute-drunk and wander the city till the early hours. Then they somehow break up even though they never were a couple, but in the end, it is all good, and they live happily ever after! That's it! Right there! The happily ever after, that is what I'm looking for. I am hoping that at the end of my drunken night there's a *pot of gold*… But it's always the *leprechaun*…

I remember once, after a long week of working I went out 'clubbing' with nobody. Just myself, out, dancing. And I did! I hopped on the stage, drank like my stomach had a hole in it. (Pretty sure it has one by now). I met this young dude outside.

"You come here a lot?" he asked coming closer.

"What do you mean? Like to the club or outside?" I came right at him with my wit.

We had a fag, shared a laugh - I thought he was cute. Not the dreamboat, nor dream anything, but for that occasion - it'd do. So, after the club, in the early hours, I went back to his student dorm. Yeah… I know. I was a bit too drunk to have sex, so he sort of fiddled around my groin with his dick, but that was the end. Us girls, we have a power of knowing if we did have intercourse or not. We can feel whether somebody was 'there'.

And so, in the afternoon, I dragged my hungover ass home and promised - never again. Well, till next time I was out. Those short-term interactions became more and more frequent. And somehow, I did not see anything wrong with it. Those were the days of *Sex and the City* glorifying women's choice of 'whenever, wherever' and *Jersey Shore* celebrating the alcohol-induced comas. So, in a way, I felt like I was being empowered rather being taken advantage off. But one guy and his words shook me straight.

It was a fabulous summer's night on a swinging Friday in Amsterdam. I was heading to my local pub for an after-work drink. The staff knew me, and I knew them since I was there every day. That's right, seven days a week. The barman on that particular night was training a new boy. Not really my type. Chubby, ginger, hairy… But the kiddo had a cracking sense of humour - and sometimes that's all the girl needs. I was about to leave, since the next morning I had a breakfast shift, as the trainee stopped me and asked for my number.

"Maybe I could ask you out?" he offered pen and a ripped piece of paper from the printer of the cash register.

"Sure! But no nude photos, please," I make a quirky joke.

I mean, why not; we can always be just great pals. Innit? As I was fishing for my phone at the bottom of my purse, I spotted the young lad I met at the club a few months ago coming in.

Since there were no follow-up messages nor second attempts - I chose to do the right thing and avoid eye contact. I waved the barmen goodbye and slid my way out of there!

At home, I sent a text to the trainee:

> It was lovely to meet you!
> How about a drink, somewhere far away from your pub?

He replied immediately with cheerful emoji and all whatnot:

> Ohhh, yes!! Haha!
> Definitely!
> This place is mental…

As I drifted away, right before I fell asleep, I thought to myself - there's something different about this one.

In the morning, rushing for my shift, I dropped him a quick *good morning* text but was a bit annoyed by not getting any message back - nothing that morning nor in the afternoon. I said to myself: *He's just sleeping, most likely finished late…*

That same evening, I sent him another text. Nothing. I was contemplating the idea of going to the pub and demanding some response - but that might come across like proper needy. The next day I texted him:

> If you are playing hard to get, well,
> you must know, it's working.

Then to my surprise, I got a reply:

> Sorry, but I really don't want to get involved with a 'hood rat'.
> Peace!

Wait! What? A 'hood rat'? What the fuck! I seriously had to google the meaning of it. And then I couldn't believe he would call me by such a name.

Then it all starts to come together. The other boy that unsuccessfully pocked me must have told him about that or something 'slightly' embellished… I was fuming. I was annoyed and crushed at the same time.

Why do men do that? Huh? Why they run their mouths like bloody girls? I wanted to disappear… There were people out there thinking of me as a 'hood rat' and the only reason why it bothered me was because, deep inside, I was afraid that it could be true. I was turning into a girl that I used to despise. I was turning into a girl that has no self-worth and no appreciation of her femininity. I was turning into a girl that nobody wants for 'the happily ever after' - and there was nothing 'glorifying' about that!

I never went back to that pub; actually, I ran away from it as far as I could. All the way to London, that is! But you know what they say - *you can run, but you can't hide.*

I was thrilled! New place - new page. Fresh start. I can be anyone! But London came with a burden on a different level.

Somehow, I managed to charm my way into one of the most luxurious hotels in the heart of London. People that knew me advised:

"Keep your personality on the low-key and just go underdog."

So, I did!

For the first few weeks, I kept it to myself; no after-work drinks, no mingling - just observation. And *boy-oh-boy* does London know how to 'deal' with the stress. Nearly all chefs in our restaurant were working split shifts, so the forty-five-minute break they'd spend outside waiting for their dealers. Cocaine is not advertised but not hidden either. I mean some guys work fifteen-hour shifts, six days a week!

When it comes to the restaurant service staff, we are a bit old fashioned, and we'd stick to liquor. Thus, if you start your shift at three in the afternoon, at about seven in the evening, the bartenders will start smuggling in the cocktails, securely disguised in takeaway coffee cups from the canteen. Believe me, by nine, you are happy to be there! Honestly, I loved every minute of it! It was like our own reality show; what sort of celebrity we will meet today, who's going to cock it up and who's going to the get biggest tips. Plus, the champagne leftovers from afternoon tea flowed freely, and I am not talking about some Cava shite. Real, French bubbles, every evening.

After a few months of 'investigation', I was entirely accepted by the team, and then, the drinking became a daily cycle not just at work, but after the shifts too. We were a team, a family! No other workplace will provide you with a community feeling like the hospitality industry will. Trust me! If you have a good team, the shifts will be more like a hang-out, just in uniform. But I did have one rule, never shall you sleep around with your colleagues! Ever! Even if you are a waitress and he's from accounts - no, don't do it - it's never going to work. Therefore, I never did. I did sleep with the guests and had terrific rendezvous with A-listers, but it's part of the gig, I guess. No regrets though! *Listen, if a certain Johnny is asking me into his room, to show me a particular acting technique, I won't be the one to say no.*

Money was coming in at a good pace and I felt like London could be the right place for me. But all went fuck up as soon as I started to look for love. Not short-term or holiday love - the real thing. That's how I encountered online dating for the very first time… That's where people met, and that's where I will meet my soul mate. You've heard the myths - they are really inspiring; two of them met on this and that website, went out and five years later got married. Everything is online these days. If I can find a good pair of high-heeled shoes without trying them on, what's the big deal in discovering real love without knowing much about that person, right?

Ian was a bit older than me, but I fancied that way (back then). We had absolutely nothing in common apart from pretending to know how to play billiards. We used to meet once a week - get drunk, play pool and fuck. In the morning, I used to fake that it was a relationship and he used to tap his fingers on the kitchen counter waiting for me to get out. Whatever that was, it lasted for a few months.

One night we were out drinking in the same pub where nobody ever goes - it was like our spot, but now I think he just did not want to be seen with me. After a few pints, we went back to his place where a flatmate of his had a couple of young girls over. I was twenty-five back then, and they were nineteen at best. But do not underestimate teens these days, man - they are bold! If they have no problem posting their butt-naked pictures on the internet, tagging their mothers in them with the title 'got it from my momma' - then they have no problem with many other things.

So, from where I was sitting, I could see that one of the younger chicks was being very familiar with Ian, and they seemed to know each other. I was continuing to drink, and an hour later, *Jack Daniel's* took over - I was pissed. From the reflection on the TV, I could see Ian standing behind my back and kissing the teenager. But as soon as I turned around, they would stop - it was like some sort of weird game. I don't know, maybe it was hot for them, but I felt annoyed. Moments later, all gitty and shite, the little slut went to the toilet. I followed the youngster inside the bathroom, pretending to want a girly chat. As soon as the doors were closed - I clutched her by the neck and slammed her body against the wall. I am short, but you would not believe what type of muscles you can get in your left arm from carrying a heavy tray eight hours a day. My hands were squeezing really hard, I was digging my thumbs into her windpipe and I felt like this could be the lesson she will 'cherish'. Her feet started to kick the wall, and Ian, from another side of the door, was asking:

"What's going on?"

The second I got distracted, she wriggled herself out if my grip. Running out of the bathroom, screaming like mad - I mean pull yourself together, right? I did not understand what the big deal was.

"Oh, my God!" she was screaming. "Call the police! She's trying to kill me!"

Nevertheless, Ian did not call the police but got me a taxi and told me to never come again. He said that I was daft and needed help. Do not remember how I got home, don't even know if I paid the taxi driver or not. I woke up in the morning - heavy, real heavy. The phone had a dozen missed calls from Ian and one text:

> She wants to press charges against you
> and is asking for your name.

I put the phone down and held my head in my hands…

"Shit!!!"

Everybody knows that if you've committed a crime and you are a hundred per cent confident that there were no eyewitnesses - deny! All of it! And never admit to it, not even to yourself.

As days followed, I met Ian for a drink. He wanted to know what had happened that night in his apartment.

"I can't believe that bitch! Why she's so dramatic?" I said.

"Dunno, but she is saying that you scared her and she is traumatised," he laughed.

"Okay, you must tell her to watch less of the Kardashians."

"So, what did happen?" Ian asked.

"Nothing! I had to pee, so I went in with her. Lost my balance and fell on her…" my previously well-practised story was 'selling' itself.

"Fair enough! I was a bit drunk too… That night was such a blur."

Being a true gentleman, he asked me for sixty-four pounds as that was what he'd paid for the *Uber* that night. Via *PayPal*, I transferred him the exact amount, and I never heard from him nor that young chick ever again. Pewww…

Okay, Ian was a mistake, and I know that now! It deeply saddens me that I wasted myself on these types of *Joes*. I would never glance at him if I were sober. *Why? Why does alcohol lower your standards?*

After that episode, I started to feel worried. I was very much aware of what happened. I confessed to myself that that night, I wanted to hurt the young girl and most likely would have done so. *And then what? Prison? What the fuck, Karolina!*

My father used to get hammered and beat the living shit out of my mom; my stepdad did the same. Later on, even my mother used to punch me - but only when drunk. Not tipsy, drunk. Then the next day none of them would ever admit to it. It's like they knew how wrong it was and that usually, it's not how they behaved. But admitting it would mean admitting to the real problem and nobody wanted to face that. Therefore - deny!

I was starting to understand that my tolerance for alcohol was reaching the level where even some men would not stand a chance. And instead of laughing, being cheeky, I started to turn violent. The smallest thing would tick me off. So, online dating stopped then and there. I also quit going out with my workmates - since I wasn't confident about what might get into me and what I might do. Hence, I'd party at home, alone. Well, not alone. *Jack* and me. *We* used to sit on the carpeted floor, smoke, drink and watch old rock-music videos. Sometimes sing and imagine that I was the next *Pop Idol.*

The devil likes drunks! He loves them. Because whenever I'm *there,* and by *there* I mean intoxicated, he comes over and offers loads of amusing things to do. Like texting your ex, booking a holiday that is too far away or too expensive, buying stuff on Amazon that you don't need, or in my case, gamble.

At the hotel where I was working, everybody was into betting, online betting. Never understood that because mainly it was orientated around sports games, but the website my colleagues were betting on had a live casino room. It's like a chatroom where you can talk to people from around the world, gamble, win or, most likely, definitely, lose. That's how it all started; one evening, I sat down with a glass in my hand, created an online account, googled some blackjack rules and concluded that now I am really *cool*. How come those ridiculous, addictive elements like alcohol, drugs, smoking or gambling make you feel like you are pretty awesome? It was quite fun to gamble online. You don't need to go anywhere, you do not need to look the part. I sat on my apartment floor, brought all the necessary booze and snacks close and stayed for hours online. I used to win, but only in the beginning because, obviously, I was able to calculate the card numbers and the points those cards stood for. But after a couple of hours, my risk assessment was non-existent, so I would lose a lot. One night I gambled away £962!

Online casinos are making billions! When you are at home, getting loaded on *Jack Daniel's*, betting left and right - there is no bouncer to come over and tell you:

"That's enough for tonight, young lady. It is time to go home."

So, you can only imagine what happened next. I lost a lot of money in one year. Money I could have saved for my own apartment or a car - I gambled it all away. I had nothing; no family that cared about me, no good friends by my side, no soul mate, no money, just a quarter of a bottle of *Jack*. That's right, I still had *Jack* in my life, and he was here to stay. *Maybe Jack was my soul mate? Perhaps living in this fermented haze is the only way to deal with life these days? Or maybe I did have a problem? Nahhh… Deny!"*

I believe that the leading reason that alcoholism thrives in this world is the fact that we are terrified to admit to it. Suppose you choose to acknowledge the presence of a problem, this would mean that you'd need to address and/or fix that problem. And of course, it would require a tremendous amount of effort. Therefore, neglecting that and just going down the same path, is much easier! No one will ever admit to a problem, till they have one!

With my hand on my heart, I did understand that I was in trouble… I truly recognised the road I was on and where it was taking me. Binge drinking is like an autobahn towards alcoholism! But I had nobody to talk to. People I associated myself with were on the same path. I felt like I needed a diversion. I wanted to turn the clock back to those school days and never take that first gulp. I wanted to blame somebody! But there wasn't anybody else to blame… I did not appreciate myself, and that's the source of all wrongdoings!

There is nothing more irritating than being out with your buddies when somebody glances at you and says:

"I believe you've had enough."

Oh, Lord, it gets my blood boiling! Or even better; you and your best friend are out in the city. Bright lights. Good vibes. The server comes, and she says:

"Oh, I will have water, not feeling like drinking tonight."

"What the fuck, Lisa?"

Listen, want to hear an honest truth? I only go out to get smashed. Period. Never understood the people that can order one glass of wine and sit the whole evening drawing imaginary circles on the tabletop with it. In my mind, what's the point of having a drink and not getting pissed? It is not that I liked the taste of alcohol. Actually, it's quite terrible. No! It's the result that I am after!

Everybody understands that alcohol has many adverse effects on your body. Women tend to get drunk faster, just because we are smaller and carry less water (since alcohol is being held not in the fat but in the body's water). But I must confess I was able to out-drink many big lads. Ten pints of *Guinness* was nothing to me. I had bartenders asking me:

"Where does it all go in ya?" and I used to gesture towards my crotch and reply:

"I do go pee a lot! It goes in and out!"

I am tiny, so when you see a small chick carrying a pint larger bigger than her own forearm, it makes you wonder.

Nobody was born with ten-pint ability, we 'train' our bodies to handle it. So, of course, year after year, my body was 'trained' to endure all the alcohol. Till the last man standing - which was usually me. But having this skill can be irritating when your friends are incompetents. That is why I started to hang out with people of my level - Polish co-workers. When you are out with Eastern

Europeans, you know that the odds of a relaxed evening are not in your favour.

The days were all the same; hangover mornings, heavy-headed shifts, lost nights on a gambling bender and if the work schedules match, never-ending Jägerbombs with *Poles.* There was no way out, no point to quit because all was under control. I had a well-paying job, a beautiful studio apartment with no flatmates, and trustworthy friends. *So, what was the problem?*

When you suffer from a severe hangover, you vow to yourself - never again. But then we make an excuse after excuse, we tell lies to ourselves justify the simple fact: you want to drink.

It was my twenty-sixth birthday, and I remember it like it was yesterday. I was out with my pals, nice bar, nothing intense. And as I was queuing for the toilet, a random guy walked up to me and said:

"Are you queuing for the loo?"

"What do you mean? It's not the line for tickets to see the new Batman film?" I replied, and he started to chuckle.

"What's the celebration for?" he nodded towards my table where my friends were being obnoxious. Also, that gave the impression that he'd been 'spying' on me for a while. I explained that it was my twenty-sixth birthday and his reply was:

"Blimey, you look like thirty-six, pet, perhaps get more sleep!" and walked away.

That comment stuck with me for a while. I looked at my own reflection, but the face that was looking back wasn't that of a budding and vibrant young woman. Not at all! There was some faint, dingy-looking gal starring back - with eyes begging for help.

But I did not know what to do or how to go about it. I was embarrassed to talk about that. Once I thought it was the appropriate moment and said:

"Do you think we should do the sober October thing?" and everybody stopped as if I'd just announced an alien invasion.

"What are you talking about? What for? We are young; we are here to enjoy London and don't forget, my dear Karolina, you only live once - just have fun!"

How can you argue with that? But I don't think I was having fun anymore. Most of the mornings I'd wake up not remembering what had happened and who this guy was next to me... It started to feel like I was repeating someone else's mistakes. Someone that I vowed not to turn into. My mother!

For those of you that did not have an opportunity to read my first book, *Let There Be Light*, you must know that my mother and I did not have an easy life. Her unfortunate decisions completely destroyed my childhood. I used to sleep in the same bed with her and her seemingly infinite number of odd men (we were renting a one-bedroom apartment, that was all she could afford, so she used to have sex, sometimes in exchange for money, right next to me! I utterly despised that period of my life). Her drinking got so severe that the blackouts she experienced were turning her into a paranoid woman. It seemed like I was in her way; she even got mad when I needed cash for schoolbooks! Her alcoholism influenced her thinking so seriously, that once she told my auntie, right in front of me:

"I should have left her on the street somewhere."

Now I know that it wasn't her talking. However, when you are a kid that just wants to be loved and nurtured, those are soul-killing words.

After many years of drinking, ultimately, she stopped. With help from prescription pills and hypnotherapy, my mother at age fifty was a recovering alcoholic. But sadly, the damage was already done. Till this very day, we keep open communications; she comes to visit, I call her every other week, but we are not your *normal* mother and daughter. You cannot build anything on top of a shaky foundation. So, we just *tiptoe* around and continue to pretend. It was hard for me to comprehend that not only did I not have a father but that the relationship with my own mother was barely existing.

Don't get me wrong, I am pleased for her that she was able to WAKE UP. She now can look back and see the mistakes, but unfortunately, there were so many that she chooses to ignore them. It is too painful for her to go back there, and I can't blame her. So, here we are; me wanting some answers and an apology and her, ignoring the past and just focusing on her wellbeing. Yes, I was feeling left out! In my selfish way, I couldn't justify why it was okay to 'wipe' it all off, all the mistakes she made, in the name of her getting better. Why should I forgive and let her move on when I am so fucking stuck! Stuck with the trauma that she caused me! Why did she deserve to get better!?

"Are you still angry with me?" she asked me once over the phone.

"I don't know how to answer that, mom."

"My therapist says that the healing will never begin till we both forgive each other," she quoted her shrink.

"Each other? What do you mean, each other?!" I was shouting.

"Well, you know, there was a time when you were very nasty to me, but I chose to heal, and I wish to forgive you." I hung up the phone because the rage inside me got me shaking.

My life was now moving in the same direction as hers was once: a large volume of booze, no money, one-night stands and absolutely zero day-to-day quality. Never being able to cope appropriately. I did what I know best; I packed my belongings and ran away from London. This time my destination was not as captivating as the metropolitan city. It was a small island in the Mediterranean Sea - Malta.

Running… Yes, that is what I do… I don't know, life was just way too complicated back then, and I did think that the only way was to extract yourself from that uncertain environment. *But was it the environment that was bad - or was it me? Was it my inability to deal with my own demons - the ones that followed me everywhere I went, like a dark cloud? Was I running for nothing, just taking all of this baggage with me?*

Malta, just like any other place, had alcohol in the shops, a big party scene and could also provide me with internet for my gambling needs. So, what I was expecting to be different? Sadly, there was nothing different. The situation was the same - I was the same. But this time around, everything became even worse…

I landed in Malta with dreams of more vigorous life, changed attitude and maybe even a possible lifetime of happiness with my very own soulmate. I was extremely pleased with the climate. My first morning coffee in December was at 24°C - I'd left London with just four degrees.

The strategy was simple: find my *Zen* and find a job. I did manage to borrow some money from my friends, just enough to give me some time to figure it all out. The rent here in Malta was a real bargain compared to the United Kingdom, and living does not cost that much either. So, I thought I'd have a couple of months. But how does one get inside a new community? You hit the local bar. At first, I visit the bar during the daytime, pretending to study the regional map and asking people around me:

"Where are the best places to visit? I've just moved here from London."

The people were really welcoming, and soon enough, I was going there for a drink every day. Evening after evening, till the money ran out and I was nowhere close to finding a job. Locals were fascinated by my lifestyle, thinking I am some sort of rich bitch with a huge inheritance. I did nothing to stop those rumours from spreading because, in a way, I enjoyed the thought of that. But I was broke and to be truthful, I didn't send out even one CV. Being too busy 'getting down with my people', I didn't bother to call the local internet company and get the internet installed. So, sending out the CVs got more tricky!

As you see, things were not improving. I was feeling lost even though I knew where I was… I felt alone in a crowded bar… And got scared of the thought that I was doing nothing.

I had nobody. I was nobody.

After shamelessly deceiving all of my friends back in England and in the Netherlands about my family's issues, I 'borrowed' more money, only this time I knew no further lies would get me through. I must find a job! And after six months of living in Malta, I finally managed to land a part-time waitressing job - not even enough to cover my rent. I guess every little bit counts - what else can you say in this situation. But I was thinking that at least all was moving in the right direction. Slowly, but moving. As time passed by, I felt more and more at home on this little island. And everything took a really good turn when I met Him!

One hot Saturday evening, I got absolutely trolleyed. Gin and tonic was my poison for the night and believe me, in the Mediterranean heat, it is delicious!

As I was making my way towards the restroom, I found a fellow using ladies. Oh, it really gets on my tits when guys do that. At first, I got scared and yelled out:

"I'm so sorry!"

But then I realised he was in MY spot, so I banged on the door and said:

"Come on, buddy, piss in your own cubicle."

Us ladies, we try to leave the loo in a decent condition for the next user, whereas boys do not care. It's like the messier, the better because wet-floor shitters symbolise how big a man you are. Grrr…

The toilet door opened, he came out with cheeks so red from the embarrassment, I found it to be adorable. He scored some points by washing his hands, and I knew I'd have to get to know him!

"Sorry," he said, and like a schoolboy caught doing something naughty, he ran out of the bathroom.

As I walked back into the main hall, he was nowhere to be found. So, I made my way towards the terrace where I spotted him smoking with another guy. I walked over and introduced myself. This, ladies and gentlemen, was THE ONLY right decision I have ever made under the influence!

His name was Ryan - a local boy. Emphasis on the boy. A bit too young for my liking, but that night I was just looking for some good banter. If only I knew then what different plan Mother Fate had prepared for me. His fair skin would never give away that he was Maltese and those blue eyes were giving me more of Scandinavian feel. Whatever he was - I found it to be very attractive!

To my astonishment, Ryan and I start seeing each other: I used to meet him after his shift at the garage, and he used to meet me once I was done 'busting the tables' at the restaurant. A few weeks later, he asked me if I would like to date him and just like that, I was in a relationship with a guy four years younger than myself, that still lived with his parents and is was allowed to stay the night. In my head, I was thinking; *I'll give it a couple of months - maximum - I can't babysit for free any longer than that.*

Ryan and I had been dating for over a year. The fact about his age was no longer bugging me because I understood that young chaps do not want to get married and have kids. Young fellas like to party, and I was definitely on it! We visited several festivals; every weekend was magical: party, people, music - I genuinely loved this Mediterranean fling. He even bought me a puppy. We named him Pooch! It's a small Chihuahua mix that locals call 'Lulu', but I am sure is just their own way of selling you a mixed breed.

Ryan worked hard all week at the garage, fixing trucks and spent weekends with me. After three weekends in a row 'outing and abouting', he said to me:

"I don't think I can do it anymore! Where do you find the energy to party every weekend? Don't you just want to relax sometimes? And just, I don't know, watch a movie or something?"

I never told Ryan that my weekend usually started on Monday.

Here, how it worked: On Monday afternoon I usually get drunk via *Skype* with my mates from the Netherlands, then on Tuesday I'm sick. On Wednesday, I often feel much better and get drunk via *Skype* with my friends from England. Then, of course, on Thursday, I am ill again. Here comes Friday and I'd meet Ryan, we would party the whole day and also Saturday. Understandably, on Sunday, I would be gone… Yes, I would squeeze a few shifts at the restaurant here and there, but I wouldn't call it work, per se.

Drinking throughout the week might not be as troubling as the amount I used to consume. The *Skype* chat would usually start with two bottles of local wine (white or red given the climate, of course), once I'd finished them, I'd usually go to find an open shop or a restaurant and buy another two… In for the kill…

The mornings after became harder and more challenging to handle. It wasn't just a hangover. I used to vomit ferociously till my insides hurt. The acid from my stomach would burn my throat, preventing me from eating for days at the time. The pain could last until the next 'occasion' - which was usually a couple of days later. And then - the same again. Over and over…

Ryan was a real lightweight. He could have five pints, and then it was over for him. So, as soon as we'd get back to my place he goes to sleep, and I'm online, looking for mates to chat with. Next thing I know it's early morning, and Ryan comes into the smoke-filled kitchen asking what time I got up - although I never went to bed… He used to wake up early and sneak back inside his house so that his parents wouldn't lecture him. I wasn't bothered! I loved my own space.

This kind of ritual was starting to affect our relationship - a lot. Even though he sort of had an idea that my drinking was troublesome, I believe he was too afraid to say anything. *I mean, have you tried telling a drunk woman that she has a problem? Oh, Sweet Lord! It's like a death wish.*

Ryan used to get really upset when we'd go out for 'one' drink, and next day we'd have plans to go somewhere and do something, but my one drink had turned into sitting till seven in the morning in the kitchen, talking with my mate on *Skype* and then not being able to do anything, but crash. He used to tell me:

"Why is it all or nothing with you? Huh? Why can't you just stop?"

And he was right! I couldn't stop. When I drank, a frenzy began, just like the vampire that thrusts his fangs into his victim's neck. The unstoppable link… And that link would only break when I had passed out!

I was ignorant. Well, maybe not ignorant, but afraid to accept it. I was a kind and loving girl, but by the time my drinks were finished, I was just a rotten bitch. Now that I look back, I wonder why he stuck by my side because I wasn't always the nicest to him. And one day, because of my drunken attitude, I called it quits.

One of those breezy summer afternoons, Ryan and I were sitting on a lovely terrace by the marina. I ordered some cocktails, and soon we both knew that it was going to be one of *those* days. As the empty glasses were removed by the waiter, and the new glasses made their way to my table, I was feeling drunk. I may have not looked like it, but I was…

Somehow, whenever I get wasted, I always end up having the same conversations; it's almost like I forget that we talked about it before, therefore, every single time I drank, we'd just end up repeating ourselves over and over and over again. Noticing the look on Ryan's face after I ordered another round, I said to him:

"Listen, pal, you do not know what it's like to be an adult. You do not know what it's like to pay rent, bills and all. So, don't fucking sit there with that judgmental look! I want to have fun and relax!"

"Why has that got anything to with it? It is not about rent and bills! We never do anything, just sit and drink. We don't go on holidays, we don't make plans. What sort of couple are we?" he snapped back.

True! Ryan and I used to talk about the future - and that subject usually scared the living *bejesus* out of me. Maybe because of the issues from my past, the nightmares and ghosts of my childhood are still pestering me. Or maybe just the sheer fear of failure - the possibility of me repeating the same mistakes as my mother did.

Ryan did tell me that, in the future, he would like to have a family; would like to have a wife and kids, but it was not something I was interested in.

When I am drunk, it's like another personality takes over! I am the queen of everything! I am the leader and the most independent creature! I do not need anyone nor anything! I am a superwoman, and I can handle it all!

"I told you many times that I want to travel, and I want to be with somebody that likes to live-it-up. I am not planning on sitting at home, washing dirty laundry and cleaning diapers!" I slurred out my words.

All of my young life, I had seen the way my mother depended on men, and I wanted none of that! Whether it be for money, companionship or protection, it didn't matter. She came across too weak and needy. Do you get where I'm going?

So, clearly, Ryan was starting to feel like he was wasting his time and me being a complete jerk, I told him to go on with his life and find somebody else to give him all these things - because I wouldn't!

That very same evening, he came over to my place to collect his belongings. That image still lingers in my memory. By far, it was one of the most unfortunate decisions that I've ever made. I was losing him. I was allowing him to walk away. With just one hug goodbye, my heart broke open, because it became apparent to me that I'd not only lost a boyfriend - I'd lost my best friend.

Ryan knew everything about me, and he never judged me. He loved me and wanted to have a future. And I chose to continue with my life, the one that I'd 'successfully' led so far! As he closed the door behind him, I lay on the kitchen floor crying uncontrollably, till I sobered up. Then I drank some more because the thought of being alone again was too much to bear.

I was never a *depressed* drinker. Meaning I used to drink only when I was feeling happy or excited and even cheeky. You know that excitement when something significant happens in your day, and you feel like celebrating? Or just an ordinary chat with a mate and reminiscences of the old days that bring out the tears of joy! I drink because I believe those moments are worth honouring! On the other hand, if I am sad, having a bad day or feeling stressed - I just want to lay in bed and sleep. I don't have the flimsiest need to talk to anybody - I just want to sleep it off!

But after my split with Ryan, it was the first time that I'd got hammered because of sorrow. And when I say hammered - I mean hammered! It wasn't just a break-up, we lived in the same neighbourhood. *So what, I have to move now? What if he starts dating somebody else? How will I handle that? What about the puppy? Will he come to visit? Should I even stay in Malta? Why would I? I don't have anybody here! Where to go? Again.*

I bought two bottles of vodka, some cheap energy drink and three packs of cigarettes - a perfect mixture for total overkill. If liver failure doesn't get me, cancer will! It was late morning as I sat in front of the computer screen, playing love tunes and feeling wretched. Once again, it was just me and the booze. My partner in crime. My dark cloud… The inebriant crutches.

The next thing I knew, it was the next day, and I was lying on my dirty bathroom floor. From the corner of my eye, I could see the dust balls under the basin unit, wriggled with my hair - because I hate to clean!

I could smell the vomit and started to realise that my lose ponytail was bathing in it. I could feel an itchiness from the dried blood all over the mouth and chin… And my small puppy lurking around and trying to wake me up because he hasn't been fed since yesterday morning. He licks my face, and I am getting disgusted by this 'picture'.

I slowly peeled myself off the floor, holding onto the sink and I looked in the mirror… *Who is this person? Why am I doing this to myself?*

That was it… I'd reached the bottom! I wasn't human anymore. I was a container, a shell. There were no emotions, no feelings - I was exhausted…

It was time!

With the hangover wearing off and a slight glimpse of clarity coming over me, I started to sense the anxiety and my fear of change. I could feel the clocks inside me shifting back to zero. I could feel the reset! I was overpowered by the need for change. A desperate appeal for a second chance. A fresh start!

Like any other person in a crisis, I turned to the only thing I knew would give me some answers - the internet. Nowadays, it's much more convenient to deal with your own drama just because other people (with more balls than yourself) put their real-life dramas online, for all of us to read, judge and learn from. I spent hours googling twelve-step programs, hypnotherapies, medical ways of quitting drinking.

Why did you not ask your mother for help? I hear you asking. My pride would never allow me to admit that I failed just like she did!

Page after page, article after article… I came across a TV series called *INTERVENTION*. I believe it's an American reality show that documents the day-to-day life of a particular addict - whether it be a drug addict or an alcoholic. The families of these people invite the production team into their home, and with the guidance of professional interventionist, they convince these troubled individuals to seek help, go to rehab and restart their lives with a clean sheet. Most of the time they fail, various relapse reasons. But the success stories are really heartwarming!

And I got hooked! I watched the episodes about the alcoholics, and in every single one of them, I saw a bit of myself; the pattern, the behaviour, the denial - the ultimate self-pity. I was in shock! Here it was, my future played by somebody else - and it's exactly how my future would look.

Some of you may say: *Big deal! You are young, you party! That's what you do!*

And the defensive, in denial part of me would agree. But if you knew someone that gambled every day, somebody that lost all his money, would you consider that person to have a gambling problem?

So, the girl that drinks herself into oblivion and uses all of her money to buy alcohol - would you agree that this girl has a drinking problem?

We have to stop downplaying the issue here! Now listen to me, and listen carefully. If you get drunk every week, and you do not recall all of the events from those nights - you have a drinking problem! Point blank! If you go out intending to get drunk - you have a problem! If thirty per cent of your earnings go to booze - you have a problem!

After three days of bingeing (pun intended) watching all of the episodes - I was horrified. I was afraid, so afraid of that show, the one featuring me, that I made a promise to myself right there and then - I will get better! I walked to the nearest stationery shop, bought a journal, opened that day's page and wrote:

00:00:00 NEW BEGINNING

I felt liberated, uplifted and somewhat restored. Back at home, I had to welcome a new life in a clean and fresh setting. I got rid of any left-over alcohol, I mopped every corner and plugged an electronic air freshener into every socket I could find. I knew it would not be easy, but I had to do it. I was so close to putting myself in a harm's way. I genuinely believe that many times as I rambled the streets at night, looking for an open shop or a bar, a guardian angel was there to protect me because I really do not know how I managed not to get mugged, raped or run over by a car.

Now that I look back and these words that I am writing years later, I can't help but feel an unbelievable amount of pride! The day I stopped drinking, I became the person I was always meant to be.

I spent some time researching articles about alcohol and the damage that comes along with it. I ticked every box in the short-term effects and the long-term damage, including unintentional injuries, alcohol poisoning, gastritis… Those were already existing binge drinking effects. And I was on the way towards liver disease, nerve deterioration…

I saw a quote somewhere that 'the odds of being involved in a drunk-driving crash - two out of three'. And 'two out of three people will be involved in a drunk-driving accident in their lifetime'. The numbers are crazy. Right? Also, people that abuse alcohol die 24-28 years earlier than people in the general population!

I cannot remember how many times I fell because I was so incoherent. How many times I burned myself, how many times I wandered around the dodgy neighbourhoods drunk and alone looking for an open shop. How many mornings I woke up to find candles still burning in the kitchen. There must be somebody above watching over me because I do not have any other rational explanation on how come I am still alive. With my drunken-wreckless attitude, come on, I could have been attacked and raped multiple times! It is shocking because I know it is true…

As we get older, the only thing we ask is for more time! More time to spend with our loved ones, more time to be around our children, more time to enjoy this life. Some of us use it well! But people like me chose it to throw it away. I did not want to be part of the hideous statistics. I knew I was ready to excel! I owed it to myself. I was a good child growing up, never asked for anything, never caused any trouble. I suffered enough, and later on, I tried to raise myself in the only way I knew how. I was a strong, hard-working young woman with tremendous potential! And I was not about to let something so stupid, like alcohol, take it all away and re-label me as a drunk!

In the history of mankind, we continuously use fear and anger as motivation tools. It helps us to steer clear of the unwanted aspects of life. I was fearful of becoming an alcoholic and absolutely furious with myself at the same time!

This type of 'cocktail' was the perfect mix for me to get better. If you feel the same, feel it! Do not hide! Be terrified and mad pissed!

I woke up the next day, right before the sunrise. As the tranquil sea right outside my window gently moved back and forth, I took a deep breath and patted myself on the shoulder. Switched on my Nespresso machine, brewed an excellent cup coffee and, for the first time in a really long time, I felt morning freshness. I opened my new journal and wrote in:

1 Day Sober

I continue to mark the journal for the next four months! It is vital to have visual evidence of your achievement. Psychologically, if you see seven days crossed off in your calendar that marks one week of sobriety, you are more likely to remain sober, because the feeling of pride and the achievement will leave you thinking: *I've done so well, why waste it!*

Feeling the excitement and abundance of opportunities, I went straight to the gym and paid for a whole year's membership! That's right - it was time! A time to get in shape physically.

You must know that I wasn't overweight nor underweight, okay. Alcohol abuse will never give things that you want or need. So, to dream about a hot body while sipping a mojito - it is not going to happen! I tried to fill my days with as many activities as I could think off. I wanted to be busy, really busy and have no time to think about drinking. I wanted to be exhausted, dead tired, and pass out (pun intended, cheeky me) on the bed the moment my head landed on the pillow. But there was one essential thing I had to do if I wanted to succeed - I had to let my friends know about the choice that I made!

I am not going to lie, okay, choosing to live sober will cost you a few friends. It is not that they do not encourage you or they aren't good friends, but for some people with similar problems, it can be hard to observe your attempt. If they are not ready to support you, don't waste your time - move on!

Once I told my so-called friends that I will need to take some time off and think about my decisions, they were supportive enough.

"Hey, it's me. Listen, it might sound strange, but I am thinking of taking a break from booze for a while. So, if I don't call you and stuff, please don't be mad, okay?" I said to one of my friends.

"Sure, I mean, it's not like we always have to drink, you know. You're the one that always starts the party. But yeah, call me if you need anything."

It's now been three years and I have no contact with any of them… And it's okay.

In the first weeks, I mainly focused on developing a clear view of my triggers; what makes me feel like having a drink? I came to realise that when I was young, I drank because of the 'cool effect'. Later on, I drank because I was lonely in a strange country. From that point on, it developed into a routine due to work, and finally, it became a habit. I avoided being alone because that would mean I'd have to acknowledge my thoughts. Thoughts about my past and how badly I was hurting inside. Therefore, I always sought company, and it came alongside the cocktail.

Once I acknowledged that pure boredom pushes me to call up mates and that leads typically towards the drinking, I decided to keep myself extremely busy. I picked up extra shifts at work, walked the dog way more then he cared for! Since I had no dependence on alcohol physically, my body felt great! Whenever the thought of a beer or glass of wine would creep in, I went straight for the fridge! That's right, baby, eat your heart out! Anything you want, cakes, ice cream, potato chips - who cares!

If on a regular Friday night, I could down ten pints of *Guinness*, that was already 1,125 calories. An average woman needs 2,000 a day, so by not drinking, I put my body through a proper calorie deficit!

You must also get comfortable with the idea of being alone - don't be afraid of getting to know yourself once again and honestly, listen to your inner voice!

The most significant help I received at the beginning of my sobriety was the teachings of *Abraham*. I will not get too much into the detail here, but I cannot stress enough the impact *Esther Hicks* made in my life! Get your hands on some of her books about the *Law of Attraction*. There are loads of videos on *YouTube* too. Please, do yourself a favour and give it a try! You can thank *her* later!

A couple of months later, I was travelling to Lithuania to renew my passport. I was thrilled to get away from the island for a bit, get a brand-new picture taken and to see my mother. The journey was planned for two because Ryan and I were supposed to celebrate my thirty-year jubilee, in my home country. I had the whole schedule planned out. Places to visit, tours, everything. I did not explain much to my mom - as in why I arrived alone. She is a very smart woman and understands that the right to know someone's personal life details must be earned.

"So, he could not come?" my mother asked as if it was not obvious. I did not say a word.

The weirdest feeling of all was the fact that I had money! Not like small change - no. I had money in my account, and that feeling was alluring! I could easily walk into a shop, buy an expensive bottle of perfume, and my card would not be declined. I could go to a Japanese restaurant, ordered whatever I fancied, and once the bill came, I would not need to check the receipt. I had the money!

I can sense you being a little bit sceptical there, so let me break it down for you. One pint of *Guinness* with blackcurrant in Malta goes for eight Euros (seven pounds, or ten dollars). On a good night, I can drink ten. That's already eighty Euros. Plus three packs of cigarettes - that's another fifteen. In one evening, I would spend a hundred Euros. That does not include my generous tipping attitude! Oh, darn… No, seriously, when I am drunk, I'd tip like stupid. As if the catering industry depends on me. It's a habit that many people who have once worked in hospitality have. *Tip your fellow worker!*

So, that was just one Friday. On Saturday mornings I'd usually go out for full English breakfast and few pints on cold cider - another thirty Euro. Later on, a date-night in a fancy restaurant, a couple of bottles of wine - another hundred Euros. I know what you're thinking: *If it's a date-night, how come you are paying for the wine?*

Ryan and I used to split every bill. And I preferred it that way. The idea of feeling gratitude to a man just because he bought me a meal or a drink, and thinking that I am obliged to spread my legs because of that - fuck off! *I'll pay for my own fish and chips, pal.*

At the end of my calculations, I found that in one weekend I used to spend around three hundred Euros. That is twelve hundred Euros a month! But that's not the shocking part… I never added the midweek drinks, the money I lost gambling… If I took it all of that into account and then multiplied it by the years I was officially employed, worked and received a monthly income - I would have been able to own my own home by now!

The anger I felt knowing that I'd literally pissed away all that money and now I'm sitting here in a bloody rented one-bedroom apartment - light up the fire under my tuchus! You too need that anger! Seriously, take your time, calculate all - you would be so enraged that the thought about spending another ten Euros on a shitty, diluted gin and tonic, would jump out of your head right away!

Now, I would like to discuss with you another example. Do you remember how afraid you were to be caught drinking by your parents? Do you remember being one hundred per cent sure that they would beat you raw? And do you remember when you turned eighteen, and your father said:

"Pour yourself a glass, why don't ya. You are an adult now!" As if you'd earned your right to drink.

You see, the world is programmed in such a way that if you choose sober living - you are useless! Useless in terms of funding.

If you go to a bar, you are not a client; you are money. If you go to a bar regularly, you are not a regular client! You are regular money! And the barmaid that is always nice to you, calls you by name and remembers what brand of whiskey you like - she could not care less about you, she cares about your money!

Do you know how many times I was in a lounge bar, and the waiter would come over to take my order and I ask for water. Do you know what I'd get? I'd get:

"You can drink water at home, luv! How about a nice cocktail?"

You and your bloody water will not bring profit to the business!

I can give you another example of a targeted audience. If you drink and you drink excessively, you are more likely to be affected and persuaded into certain purchases or spending. Friday night and an advertisement comes up on a popular music video channel, with a very cheery voice:

"This Summer! Your favourite music channel is bringing you a party like never before! Good people! Good music and never-ending celebration! Get your tickets now!"

And in this commercial, you will see some extraordinary and enticing shite like: sexy and loose women, icy cocktails, beautiful scenery. You, of course, will go ahead and look on the internet at where to buy the tickets. They will charge you €399.99 for a VIP ticket and offer *Meet and Greet* for another €199.99. Then, the next morning, you will realise that you still need to pay your own airfare!

There are no commercials on Friday nights for vacuum cleaners. If there were, my apartment floor would be spotless!

And finally - the industry. Every establishment that serves food and drinks knows that the money comes from the beverages and not the food. Once the owner calculates the cost of the food and preparation, the profit is not as high compared to what comes from the beverages. A cup of tea? Two Euros. How much does one teabag cost?

See it for yourself! Go to a restaurant, order bottle of water, and you will get no attention whatsoever, even though you ordered the most expensive steak! Go to another one and tell the waiter to bring the most expensive bottle of wine and you won't be able to get the manager's nose out of your butt!

I worked at a posh restaurant. There we were taught how to upsell, and we'd get rewarded for that!

"Would you like to start with an apéritif?" your waiter will ask. And he will tell you the story about how a bitter cocktail is a great way to activate the taste buds. And you know it's bullshit because you're not supposed to drink anything thirty minutes before your meal, so the acid in your stomach would remain at its perfect potency.

"Would you like to order a bottle of white with the starters and red with your mains?" he will be pushing. And you know its rubbish because the fermentation in the stomach must remain undiluted therefore you should not even drink water with your meal.

"How about a digestive drink?"

What is this place? you'll think, *a restaurant or a doctor's office!* They are professionally trained for days at a time to make your dining experience unforgettable! And you will remember it forever because, after paying that bill, you will starve for the rest of the month.

I am not declaring that there is a worldwide conspiracy rolling around you to keep you sedated. I am merely pointing out that the new world is designed to get the most cash out of you - and it is easier to do that if you are a drinker!

It's been officially one hundred days that I've been sober! I remember standing on my balcony, watching the sea and being overwhelmed with pride. No more injuries, no more hangovers. No more night-time calls from strange numbers at and even stranger voices asking to come over. No more mess. No more regrets. No more self-pity! *I did it! All on my own.*

My self-centred thoughts were interrupted by an incoming text. I looked at the screen of my phone. It was from Ryan!

> Hey, how is it going?

My heart was pounding. I texted back:

> Hey, I am wonderful, thank you, how are you?

A few minutes later, his response was:

> Glad to hear. I miss the dog, can I come and see him?

My face started to flash, and I did not know what to do or how to reply to that. It was evident that my panic had taken long enough for Ryan to send another text.

> It's okay. I understand if you don't want to see me…

> I texted back:
> No! I mean, yes, you can come! When?

> Can I come over now?

I looked in the mirror: the biblical cold sore was traversing over my upper lip, my hair was greasy, and the bathrobe I was wearing was smeared with barbeque sauce, that frankly looked like poo.

> Sure! Come over.

I pressed SEND and rushed to tidy up the kitchen.

As soon as I saw him in front of my door, my heart plummeted… I'd missed him so much, and now I wasn't able to suppress my emotions. He came over and hugged me as my tears were streaming down my cheeks. I told him about my sobriety, and he was extremely pleased for me. That night he stayed over. All night… And he's never left since.

During my first year of sober living, I lost a dear friend. He and I were childhood friends, we did everything together, and when I decided to live in the Netherlands, it broke us apart. We kept in touch, but I wasn't in the right place. He religiously practised yoga and chose a clean lifestyle *way* before I did. So, our ability to connect on the same level wasn't there. We lost each other as friends, and I was very keen to re-introduce myself to him. I was too late... My friend passed away in his sleep at the age of thirty-two on the day of his birthday. I never sent him a message, always thinking: *I'll send him one tomorrow.*

I cried like I haven't cried in a long time. I was overwhelmed and in disbelief that somebody who would appear on my *Facebook* timeline every day, had disappeared forever. That's how it is nowadays; we do not feel like we need to be in touch since we are *following* their online lives... Such foolishness.

Luckily, my grief was not accompanied by alcohol. I was very much aware that it's a sign of the weakness and I should not numb my emotions, but rather experience them! It was the time when I understood that I was officially 'out of the woods' and I was not slipping back into the same pitfalls.

It will take some time to build new, sober memories, so you might struggle a bit in the beginning. You will reminisce about the times and the fun you had at *this* party or *that* club, and you might feel like it is not worth it. But trust me, the new memories you'll make will be remembered by you for far longer than the drunken ones.

And if you will slip, it is not a big deal! Recognise that! Analyse why and how come! Dare to step into that dark place where the need for numbing lies and ask the questions. And of course, take one step at a time! I cannot stress enough the importance of 'taking it easy'. Focus on one day, just today, and you will see how easy it will get as the days go by. Find some support; maybe it's a friend (a non-drinking one), or a family member. Don't be afraid to share your journey with somebody, because the people that love you and wish the best for you will have your back!

But let me be very clear, if you are not ready, nothing will work. If you are thinking: *I really wish to stop drinking, but I can just spend weekends at home!*

It will not work!

If you are saying to yourself: *Okay, I do get drunk on the weekends, but it is not a big deal.*

It will not work!

If you believe that you are in danger due to high and frequent alcohol consumption, you will get better!

The next very healthy thing to do is to write a gratuity journal. You can write on a notepad or get yourself one of those really cute looking journals. Some like to type on their phones. No matter which way you choose to capture your gratuity, you have to be able to go back and review it once in a while.

It doesn't need to be long, it can be just a few lines, but really focus on things for which you feel appreciative. I write my journal every day! In the morning, once I am back with my dog, I sit down, sip my coffee and take it all in. I give thanks for a well-rested night; for the lovely morning and the healthy body that I woke up in. I give thanks for the lovely tasting coffee and the faithful *Starbucks* mug that makes it extra tasty. I give thanks for the beauty I get to see around me.

Do not, I repeat, do not focus on the negative aspects or lack of some sort! It will only make your recovery more difficult. Let them call you ignorant! Be absolutely oblivious of the negatives! The stronger your appreciation gets, the less tempting alcohol will become, simply because your life will be everything you ever wanted it to be! Appreciation will allow you to get your focus back on how many beautiful things you have in your life. And once you acknowledge this, the rest will follow.

As much as I was satisfied with my ability to remain sober, I was still a smoker. Back then, I was accustomed to smoking three packs in one day while drinking - I would smoke none on my hangover days. But now, I was smoking a pack a day - every day! I knew that my frustrations were looking for some sort of alternative escape. There is nothing more pathetic than a drunk woman than a woman that reeks of cigarettes!

Since the internet was such a great help during my search for sobriety advice, I went back and asked almighty *Google*:

How to quit smoking?

The amount of information was overwhelming, and it looked like every article contained a guarantee of success… This time I wasn't sure, so I called my mom and asked:

"How did you manage to quit smoking?

Oh, you smoke?" she asked me as if she did not know.

"Erm… Yes, sometimes."

Even being a grown woman myself, I still can't stop lying to my mother.

"Well, I read this book and never smoked since!" My mom told me the name, but I will not mention it here.

I bought the book and read it, and it's shite! A complete waste of twenty Euros, which in my world is four tubs of *Ben & Jerry's* Chocolate Fudge ice-cream! The internet was raving about this book, and I absolutely believe that maybe ten years ago it was revolutionary - but it did not make any sense now.

And so, I went to my General Practitioner for advice. She prescribed me a little blue pill (not that one) and it was supposed to stop the cravings. It wasn't cheap (I believe in England you can get it for free via the NHS) but I wanted to quit really badly, so I paid!

One pack contained fourteen pills - for the first two weeks. I took the first one and felt ill the whole day. I had no other cravings but to stick my head in a toilet and puke my intestines out! After finishing the two-week course, I did not want to buy another pack, and, against my doctor's recommendation, I threw the prescription away.

Soon enough, I was celebrating my one-year 'soberversary' and two months of smoke-free life! And I haven't smoked since!

Was there a time I felt like smoking? you ask. Hell yeah! But as I was looking at the calendar with all those days marked in red, I could not wipe it all away as if it did not matter!

Next to the calendar, I also created what I call a 'Good Girl Jar'. In this simple, glass jar (I think it was a pasta or cereal jar) I was putting in seven Euros - every day. For each day I did not smoke a pack of fags, I would put in cash and see it 'grow'. At the end of the month, I took the money out (nearly two hundred Euros) and bought myself a dress. Because that was money I did not spend on killing myself; therefore, it would be spent on celebrating my choices!

If you are a smoker and wish to quit, try the jar! You would be amazed by the feeling you'll get when you treat yourself, right!

With the money that I succeeded in saving up, I periodically set some aside and paid off all of my debts. At first, it was tough to resist the temptation of spending it all on an exotic holiday - but I knew that I'd thank myself later.

You see, when you quit drinking for long enough, your brain retrieves the ability of thinking in such a systematic manner - you would be amazed. When your mind is clear, you will take the time to consider all aspects. When your mind isn't highjacked by alcohol or drugs, you can take time and assess the information. And this, my friend, will allow you to make the right decisions!

You do not need alcohol! Simple! For you to survive and maintain a functioning body and mind, alcohol is not essential. It contains no valuable nutrition that your body cannot get from somewhere else! (A while back, there were some studies done to determine benefits from the ferments found in red wine. I am slightly sceptical about that study since I cannot find who was funding it. So, if you get to read those 'articles' about the benefits of tequila, just keep on reading…) It is just something that you were introduced to, offered, and now the world is forcing you to believe that you need it. But you don't! Think of alcohol as some sort of traditional dish from a foreign culture that you'd never heard of and never tasted. You were capable of living all of your life without it. So, if you had never come across booze, you would be able to live just fine!

But we hear those tales about the man that drinks a glass of red each day and has never been to the doctor! I hear you protest.

There is absolutely nothing wrong with enjoying a glass of wine, sipping on a good whiskey, or treating yourself to a beautiful glass of *Champagne*! Nothing at all! That is not the point. My point is, when you start to look for answers in booze, you will fail!

I took my time to identify the source of my drinking. I understood that whatever had happened to me in my childhood, I had not recovered from it. And being afraid to deal with it, I medicated myself with alcohol. And with years of that type of 'therapy', I did not know anything else. I did not know how to be alone, how to depend on my own abilities as a person and as a woman.

The pressure nowadays is ridiculous! You can discover something wrong in every aspect of this modern life, but that will get you nowhere. We must stop looking 'outside' and clear the shite from within. When you have that inner peace, you can do anything you set your mind to! I can promise you that! Everything starts from within; health, happiness, love, money - everything.

We've all heard about the 'Dry Law'. If you haven't… in the 1920s the USA government issued a new law that stopped all manufacturers of alcoholic beverages from manufacturing, releasing and selling booze! That way, the government thought they could end crime and poverty in the country. Obviously, it did not go as planned, but that is not important.

If you read magazines, you may not realise that a big part of those well-written articles may be nothing but an advertisement. For example:

A 100-year-old veteran claims that a small whiskey once a day is the secret to a long life.

And then somewhere around that article, there's going to be a picture of some fancy whiskey brewery. Big companies pay big money to newspapers and magazines to release absolutely bogus material like that - just to sell their products.

Go ahead, type into *Google*:

Alcohol and its effect on health

Come on! You will find an endless number of articles explaining in-depth about the possible danger of alcohol and its deadly effect. But you will also find a sentence like:

...while the occasional glass with dinner isn't a cause for concern...

The health organisations cannot come and say:

Any amount of alcohol is harmful. If you drink a spoonful of vodka, it's kaput to you.

If they did, most of the governments would be forced to close the factories, shops, stop imports and exports. People would lose jobs, and the economy will feel its toll.

I will repeat this again, there is absolutely, one hundred per cent, totally nothing wrong with having a drink. For instance, you and your friends, at the campsite, by the fire, playing the guitar and singing good old tunes. You are having a beer, having a laugh and enjoying this moment. Later on, you go to sleep, you have a restful night, you wake up and do whatever you camping types do.

Or, you and your buddies went out to watch a game, you drank a couple of glasses of whiskey. You got home, ate, showered and in the morning you feel nothing, and you go to work as usual.

That is an acceptable drinking behaviour!

Since Ryan and I share the same household, sometimes when he's off from work, I compose a 'do it whenever you can, but better now, otherwise I'll give you an evil look' list. Things to fix around the house. Ryan told me dozens of times:

"I can only remember one thing a day. That's my limit."

So, if I ask him to change the lightbulb in the hallway and fix the mosquito net, one of these two requests will be overlooked. But, just like any other man trying to get in a kerfuffle with the woman, he's developed a bizarre but powerful technique: he would go ahead and start changing the light, but to remember about the mosquito net, he takes the inside of his pocket and pulls the material out! So, as he goes about his day, once he notices the pocket hanging outside of his trousers, Ryan would immediately know that he was meant to fix the net! Once the assignment is complete, he shows the pocket right back in - and we are living a hassle-free life!

Equally, it would help if you have a symbol of some sort to remind you about your decisions and your sobriety. Will it be a beautiful watch, ring, bracelet - maybe even a tattoo! Something to look at daily and remember why you are doing this and acknowledge how much you are accomplishing! Seeing a positive reminder of your lifestyle will only boost your mood and uplift your spirit even more!

As I watched my body growing stronger and more robust with every workout, I also lost ten kilograms! Weight loss is another great benefit of sober living! I was feeling powerful, mentally and physically! To test me, I signed up to run in Malta's International Marathon. I had no intention of running the full one - that is something that only un-humans, alien-type creatures can do! I stuck with the 'half'.

I trained every day. I ran short distances fast, long ones at a slower pace. There was no competition because when you run a marathon, you run for yourself.

There will always be somebody better than you, so why bother? My aim was to cross the finish line in under two hours, and at 1:59:43, I finished my race with a definite feeling that I was going to die… My body ached, there were blisters in between every toe and I will never do this again! I wanted to prove myself and to punish myself at the same time. I needed to punish myself for abusing nature's gorgeous creation with years of smoking and drinking.

If you think that you cannot quit drinking or smoking, I can only advise you to try. Do not think about the birthday you have to attend and how people will think it's strange. Do not think about that project you must finish and how stressful it will be. Do not think about that New Year's party that you have been invited to and that the temptation will be too strong. Just focus on today. One day at a time is the perfect pace for you. If you manage to stay healthy and happy today - that is it! You've done it! Because tomorrow, well, you might not live to see the dawn… Sorry to say that, but none of us knows when the time will run out. So, concentrate on today.

I cannot guarantee that this book will bring you all the answers you might need. But I can guarantee you this:

If you are drinking enough to experience blackouts - you will make terrible decisions!

If you are drinking too much and too often - you will never have enough money!

If you are drinking because you're hurting - you will never get better!

If you are drinking because you feel stressed - you will never be at peace!

If you are drinking and you cannot stop - it will kill you!

There's a saying in Lithuania:

Life is like a museum. You can walk around, experience the beauty, enjoy what it has to offer. But you cannot take anything with you on your way out.

Every day you have a choice about how you wish to live your Life! Every day you are given the opportunity to accomplish more, do more and be better! You were given this life to experience all that you wish to! And it is funny how we waste this valuable time on activities that do not matter, on people that aren't worth it. Time was given to all of us. We don't know how much of it we have, but the older we get, the more precious it becomes. And alcohol will only erase it!

You must agree that no recovery can take place if a person is still in denial. In the name of getting sober, you must admit that you are no longer in control of your drinking. If you can relate to some of my stories, if you can make the connection - you, my friend, are on the path to self-destruction. But if you are ready to acknowledge the situation, if you are willing to give yourself some time - you will be an example to others!

Start slowly. Decide that this week you are not drinking and engage in some other activities. Spend some time and write down all the possible triggers for your drinking. Start documenting your thoughts of gratitude in a journal and really pay attention to your feelings.

But I work at the bar. How can I avoid the triggers? you ask. Well, I am not a genie, I won't jump out as soon as you open the book, and I will not take you by the hand to drag away from all temptation. The world will never stop offering you the opportunity to take a *bite of the apple*. You must be sure of yourself and strong enough to walk away. If your mates are asking you to go out for a drink, just reply:

"No, thank you. I am trying to stop."

If this sentence is greeted with laughs and jokes - they are not good mates! Listen to me very carefully, no active, in denial, alcoholic will be genuinely pleased for somebody else's sobriety! If you acknowledge the problem and those are the people that you used to drink with, it could mean that they have the problem as well. Therefore, your sobriety will be a constant reminder of their possible problem!

Only the people who are truly there for you will embrace your choice and give the support that you need. But I have news for you; if you are in a relationship with a person that shows more or less the same symptoms of addiction as you, and that person does not recognise it as a problem - it will not work out! Sobriety will not be possible to achieve, or the relationship will fail - there is no other way.

During the first year, Ryan did not drink or smoke anywhere near me. He still went out for a pint with his friends, never came home drunk nor tipsy. He would go out saying:

"Going for a pint and burger."

...and comes back after drinking one pint and eating his burger. He can enjoy one drink, and that is how it should be. Now I do not have any triggers, so if we are dining at a restaurant and he orders a glass of wine - I could not care less. *But no kissing till he's brushed his teeth!*

We have all just experienced an unusual phenomenon - a lockdown. Some of us came out of it as a better version of the person we were, some of us did not. This is a perfect time for you to take that time and distance yourself from everything that you identify as your triggers. You could not think of a more ideal moment than right now. You don't need to go out, you don't need to see anybody - the hell, you don't even need to admit your addiction to others, if you are not ready!

It's a perfect storm. So, go ahead and take your chances!

Okay, I do not wish to across as a world-class douche, but when you lead a sober lifestyle, you do get a feeling of superiority over others. Before you got all frantic, please, just hear me out.

Problem-solving is a skill. It's a skill that each of us possesses, yet we express it on different levels. Some of us are better problem solvers than the others. We all know that person you can reach out to for a piece of advice, and blimey, that person is usually right!

When you numb your brain with some sort of sedative (drug, alcohol, magic marker, computer duster, etc.) for the time being, your ability to think clearly is paralysed. And with more frequent numbing, the brain, just like a muscle you no longer use, gets weaker and weaker. And that is why people that suffer from addiction continue to make bad decisions because their 'thinking muscle' is no longer strong enough to offer a better solution.

If you decided to buy a house, you would go for advice to a person that knows the industry. When you want to purchase a particular car, you go to a mechanic and ask for his opinion. When you want to stop drinking, you go to somebody that already stopped. You cannot go and try to get advice on this matter form somebody that drinks. Only a recovering alcoholic, like me, can tell you what to do.

So, what should I do? you ask. Just don't drink. That's it… You are not asking yourself to do something; you are asking yourself not to do something. Think about it as if I had asked you to run forty kilometres - that is a hard shite to do! Not running would be the easy thing to do, no? So, how comes not doing something can be hard?

It's a pattern, a habit, and you just need to focus on it and change that pattern, break the habit. One day at a time!

And so, when you succeed in being sober and live your life while observing your surroundings - you will feel a sense of pride and superiority over those that sit and weep their troubles into a bottomless flask. Being able to deal with pressure and stress without any 'sedatives' is a superior quality. Being able to make the right decisions and consider all possibilities is a valuable skill to possess.

Without the daily, weekly dose of those 'sedatives' as I call them, your brain 'muscle' will continue to work for you. Kids do dumb shite because they don't know any better (yet). Drunks do dumb shite because they 'forgot'.

Ryan and I have already been together for five years. If I hadn't made the decision to get sober, we would not be together at all. That would not have been possible! Because of my drinking, I nearly lost the most beautiful gift in life - love. Because of my fear of being honest with myself, I was close to losing my best friend.

How about the future? I hear you asking. As I was taking the time and analysing my thoughts, it became clear to me that I wasn't afraid of getting married and having children. I wasn't scared of repeating my mother's mistakes. No. I was scared that I would need to do it alone! That was my bogeyman. I could not imagine raising a child on my own. I could not imagine the heartbreak of a divorce! But when I allowed myself to understand that with the right person by my side, through better or worse, for as long as we both shall live - I do not need to be afraid. I wasn't alone anymore!

Life goes on, and every day I discover something new about life, the world, myself and the surroundings. I prefer to look at the good and not bother with the bad. With every passing day, I understand how quickly the time is vanishing, and there is nothing I can do to stop it. You cannot buy time! Well, no, that's a lie… You can do one thing that will buy you some time - wear sunscreen!

As for my sobriety, I've stopped counting the days. I am sober, and I choose to remain this way for the rest of my life. Ryan did ask me once:

"Do you think you will be able, one day, just to order a drink and that's it?"

"What for?" I said, "alcohol is pointless, expensive and actually not that tasty!"

I order non-alcoholic beer once in a while, just to taste that particular bitterness, but that is it. If we go out, I have tonic water and watch the rest of the patrons wasting their time…

Epilogue

As the line on the cover of this book tells, this is my final one. No, it is not the Michael Jackson trick. You know, when you announce your retirement, and then a few years later you start a 'Come Back' tour… It is not like that, this really is my last book.

But why, you are so gifted! I hear you object. Yes, I am! But all the kidding aside, misery does love company. Us humans, we adore the bad story turned good. We feel a greater connection with those that failed because we can all learn from mistakes, mine, yours… I am in a very happy place! And I choose to stay here. Frankly, I do not think I would be able to ramble on and write a hundred pages about my happiness. Who would read it anyway…

Sometimes, I ask myself: *Would I go back and change it?* I don't think so. I am afraid that for me to become who I am now, I had to go through all of this gross tar-like life. I'm scared that if I change one event in my past - I wouldn't be this person that I am. And maybe because I was a broken girl, I was able to become a 'whole' woman.

Over three years ago, I stopped the clocks and announced a new time - *My Time*! I do admit it wasn't easy, but it was bloody worth it. Hopefully, you can embrace the change and announce *Your Time* too!

We are living in a world with all the information we need at our fingertips. And, if you ever want to talk - I am easy to find! Drop me a message if you succeeded, and I will cheer for you! Drop me a message if you failed and I will support you! Drop me a message if you're afraid and I will encourage you! *But no nude photos, please!*

And if you ever find yourself in Malta - drop me a message. Coffee's on me!

Goodbye,

Sincerely yours - Karolina

Also by Karolina Robinson

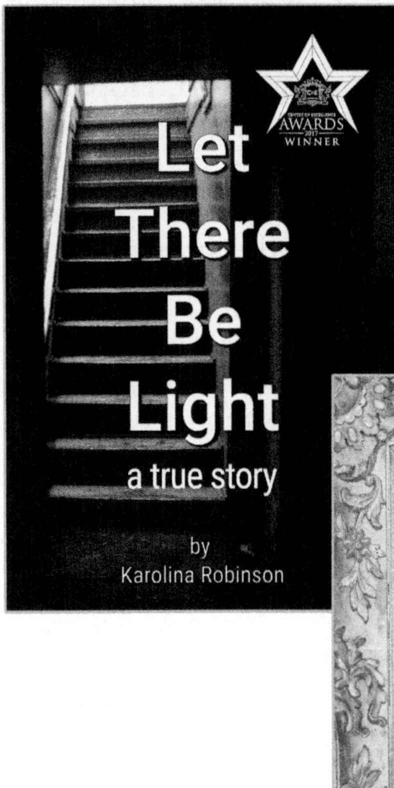

More at http://viewauthor.at/KAROLINA

You can always share your thoughts with me:

https://www.facebook.com/robinson.karolina

Also, join me on my *Youtube* channel where I talk about spirituality and awakening:

www.youtube.com/c/LoAwithK